THE POETRY OF PETE HAWKES

Poetry to Help You Survive the Modern World

Contents

The Rat Wheel

Roll up roll up, watch the rat wheel spin round and round.
If you press the button to get off, the money stops flowing down.
Yet I stay on the wheel so I can collect my precious PAYE.
Alas my home loans and taxes just take it all away.

And my rat wheel friends are just the same.
And like a morning plague we board the train.
Now just a sequence of numbers we've long forgotten names.
We all dream of Friday where we can drink and complain.

I know yesterday and tomorrow are just the same day.
My colors all run dry - I can only see grey.
Brainwashed since youth "all work and no play",
we will all have better super wont we, the longer we stay.

Here on the rat wheel,
we're treading as fast as we can,
trying to overtake the richer man.
But as fast as I tread, I never seem to get ahead.
So much faster and harder next week I must tread.

All the pigs grunt and squeal in their own personal pigsty.
And not one little piggy dare chance a new life to try.
Nazgûl's they are - neither living nor dead but wanting to die.
Hypnotically seduced by the rhythm of the rat wheel's lie.

The Journey Out of Depression

Was that a faint willow whisp of light?
It's dancing to and fro like some mischievous devious ballerina, dangerously playing
games with the night.

I am utterly mesmerized and spellbound.
Who is this lunatic that dare come around?
Please, l am comfortably inert, happily deserted and hurt,
l insists, let me stay down.

But no, no, rather, it taunts me, it haunts me, there's some sacred secret spell, l feel an inner
glow, like l am somehow strangely hollow. l am compelled, l am seduced, l am reduced, l
resist but cannot desist, somehow, inevitably l am required to follow.

Suddenly my eyes are filled with unbearable light.
It's an agony so beautifully wonderfully bright.

Now free. I can see! I have sight! slowly my deepest depression fades,
a window is growing in that eternal tomb, my womb of darkest night.

Free from bondage, my mind has motion. Suddenly l have emotion.
It's like being born again or drinking some kind of magic potion.
Elation and commotion. Void to devotion.
A sea of rainbows becoming a euphoria of oceans

Dreams run wild and cascade like waterfalls in my mind,
and all it needed was a little time.

A Violin's Sweet Note

With gentle loving caress the violin and bow were united.
Their union created a child,
so delicate, so melodic, the parents delighted.

I watched it in its infancy, as it floated into the incandescent sky
and the cry of her first breath left me speechless,
my mind numb, my mouth dry.

For the muse is a sculptor who medium is not stone
but rather the very midnight air,
and this was a Michelangelo of sound,
a simultaneous contradiction in joy and despair.

For the joy came first when she knew she was finally alive
But despair was the note deeper down when soon after,
she was aware, she would not long survive.

And even though she would live only for moments, doomed to die,
I will always remember the sounds of her birth.
That exquisite evocative melancholy cry.

The Executive Meeting

Another meeting.
The anticipation.
Come all ye vacant suits of suave sophistication.

Another perturbation.
Another presentation.
But no one saved.
No salvation.
Just more bullshit, politics, and masturbation.

Borrowed Time

I thought once we never left
but the truth is we lose a little life with every breath.
slowly, yet surely it creeps, everywhere, every day we see the signs
as we live out our lives on borrowed time.

So we wake and remember but ignore the pain,
we welcome another winter and dance dreams in the rain
and life goes on being cruel, wondrous, and even sublime
while she happily counts us down on our borrowed time.

And so the meter is running, yet the music's still yours
so, go on, write your life in six eight, waltz or standard four four
but whatever you choose, leave just a little behind
don't waste your precious precarious borrowed time.

I thought once we never left
but now I know the truth about life within death.
With no reason, no rhythm, no warning, no rhyme
it's like we never did exist, not even our belated bubble of borrowed time.

Mirror Mirror

Mirror mirror on the wall,
seems like even time you can stall

As every time we meet,
I have a little less hair and am a little more aged
I notice by contrast, you silent immutable fuck,
that you never change.

The Day

The day has come, see how the rainbows greet the water,
watch the vivid crimson light of dawn: The world is reborn.

Smell the crisp air after the midnight rain,
look at the delicate drops of dew: everything, everywhere, is new.

I will not waste this day!
It is the last today that will ever rise.
I must farewell the sunset, dance in the midnight moonlight,
wonder in awe at the sacred sunrise.

And if the universe is an ocean then this day alas,
is but one watery drop of time.
Still 1 will remember her forever.
So majestic, magnetic, magnificent, and sublime.

I Rob, I Robot

Artificial intelligence, emotional cripple.
No tremor of joy, not even a ripple.

No connection, no passion, no elation,
just a computerized mechanical mind,
what a strange combination!

One yearns to tell, cos he's missing it all.
The earthquakes of laughter, the friendships,
the parties, the fun of it all.
But you'd be wasting your time and wasting his.
Because a robot cannot compute human bliss.

But he's very cognoscente his time is finite?
So one thinks eventually he'll see the light?
Ironically, being programmed for detail he's lost all sight,
and so tragically before even starting, he's lost the fight.

And It's strange to me that l have found,
that it's the artists who don't seem want to hang around.
The candle burns bright but burn out fast,
ever giving back, they don't care they last.

But the ones who want to live forever,
never leave behind a single endeavor.
Looking after their health, like their God's own treasure,
they live a life that has no worth or measure.

So work and worry, struggle, and strife,
win the promotion, lose your wife.
Keep focusing on trivial, minor, useless trite
congrats...you've well-earned your useless, petty, nothing life.

The Empty Vessels

Beware those who would scream in the silence of the night.
Who need a crowd, who require the white-hot spotlight.

They walk the earth as empty vessels, all shell and little soul.
Being all production with no content,
like a living, breathing David Letterman's show.

And while they big note themselves on the purchase of their seventh house, their soul
remains timid, frightened, unsure, quiet as a mouse.

Elaine

Even if it's a whispered scream or a trivial devastation,
with her it evolves into either murderous madness or exhilarating elation.
See how she shakes dreams from her hair like rainbows of gold, like wild magical rain. The
colors never run grey with that dreamer Elaine.

The curves so perfect, they set men's hearts burning.
The mystery needs fulfilling, and their desire ever so yearning.
The attraction so strong, so as to explain, please beg my pardon,
but the way Elaine looks she could give even a paraplegic a hard-on.

So watch her walk away, watch her ignore your advances
She already knows the question, happily smiling,
she leaves you no answers.

And the last image that now fills your one tracked brain,
is of her shaking dreams from her hair
like rainbows of gold, like wild magical rain

And even deep down if you could so burrow, even then could you explain
the heart and mind and soul of Elaine?
But like all great mysteries unknown even from the days of old
The paradox of Elaine is left better unsolved.

Ah... so you've tried to forget, but your still wounded and maimed.
Now your trapped now like so many before you in her spiderweb game.
And those dreams now become nightmares, played over and over again.
Was there ever a man who could forget the memory of Elaine?

The Probability of Destiny

My fate, my destiny,
If you're a quantum man show some fealty,
For even certainty they say is but only aggregated chance?
certainly, nothings for certain, for they say even
nature is just a moving random dance?

So what now?
Am l choosing here and there,
like a particle in this verse?
Or are my actions useless and perverse?

Has fate foretold my future -it's already decided?
Are my ideas worthless and derided?
Is time merely an illusion as Einstein says,
or is it the aggregated sum of millions of waves?

Somehow l think somethings missing,
like nature is screaming out the answer but no one's listening.

Something on the grass is yellow and glistening
These were my thoughts while l was casually pissing.

People

Short, fat, skinny troubled, anxious, disturbed,
angry, frustrated, lonely, perturbed.

This is the view from my window seat
the morning hustle on the Melbourne street

The True Asshole

Don't you just love the true asshole,
they could promise you heaven in hell.
Watch for telltale signs, the soft touch, the hard sell.

Emotions and love,
for them just a game habitual.
The care and trust on display,
a carefully practiced ritual

Wax lyrical they will of their conquests and glories in the days of old.
Your treated like royalty,
you don't know it yet,
but you've already been sold.

And it is a well-known fact is that the true asshole
at a distance can never be smelt,
but up close its unbearable,
and the practiced plastic emotions slowly start to melt.

And eventually, once you know them,
their true colors finally shine through,
hideous black, drab grays,
blood red in splattered, treacherous backstabbing hues.

And deep down somehow you want to forgive them,
and you ask yourself why?
Is it because I suspect, the story behind every true asshole
would make a grown man cry.

Light at The End of The Tunnel

You've been kicked when your down, spat on by the human race
When one door closes another always slams in your face.

Don't forget there's light at the end of the tunnel,
always hope of a new day.
But then you realize this light is in fact just another train
directly coming your way.

So your stuck in depression, in your tunnel doomed to die.
The train is so fast, your trapped, you say your final goodbye.

But the train doesn't kill you, you wake in hospital, and you're so glad you've survived.

And to your surprise you're now a crippled paraplegic with only one eye

What Will You Do?

With lightning speed, we are transformed from the cradle to the grave
Having nothing more at death than at birth other than
our sacred soul to be saved

No deed no action will ever change this inevitable outcome God ordained
But will tragic truth really change your life's view?
Now you know your finite, what will you do?

The Star-Spangled Manner

America, home of the brave, land of the free
Or is that home of the slave, land of the fee
They franchise their culture to the world
as something wonderful we need
A mixture of porn stars, McDonald's and pay TV

The Taliban, so evil, it's so obvious, it's so black and white
But let's not forget it was America who supported the Taliban
in the Afghan Russian fight

And we have to get Saddam, stop the villain using the WMD
before he makes a start,
but you get no prizes to guess which county
supplied him with all the component parts.

What do you mean you found no WMD?
we know they are there... search every street.
We know he's making them,
he's just hiding them; he's obviously being very discrete!
And if you still can't find them,
we can prove they exist, it's a simple feat,
just see our Pentagon accountant, let him show you the receipts.

Our presidents are so talented, so intellectually fulfilled,
But George W Bush still complains
'it's hard to be president these days as you have to be so multiskilled'
Depressed he confesses, 'I'll never able to answer the phone and simultaneously get a blow
job like good ol' Bill'

Now good ol' bill, slick willy, now he didn't fail.
Well, OK he did in policy, but not with the millions of women he nailed.
And they say Bill was a drug addict, but this is an unfair portrayal,
because we all know that good ol' bill never lied, and he never inhaled.

There is truth and there is Justice, and then there is the American way.
I'll give you a discount on your freedom, provided you pay cash by today.
And we believe in honor, integrity, and democracy, just so long as you pay.
Morally and financially bankrupt, they have long since their day

America, home of the brave, land of the free
Or is that home of the slave, land of the fee
They franchise their culture to the world
as something wonderful we need,
A mixture of porn stars, McDonald's and pay TV.

One Day Saved

The tranquility of having time,
no morning train, no stress,
no getting up to make a dime.

Walking in my house in trackies and ugg boots.
No dressing like a slave, no bloody tie and suit.

And I can see my friends and I can smell the flowers
No trivial bullshit meetings with corporate wankers at the Rialto towers

And I expect one day when your close to reaching the grave,
You'll be happy that at least this one day you did save.

The Record Company Executive

As I watched I saw a vision of a shark with a crocodile's smile
what emerged was no less strange:
a walking talking asshole with infinite guile.

In front of me, without a doubt stood
the best used car salesman in the land.
I speak of none other than the record company executive,
that genuinely shonky man.

"Pete your unique what a wondrous sound,
what a great and fabulous talent I have found,
there's no one like you, we will make rivers of gold,
promise me your song I promise thousands of copies sold".

So I left weary and worn but signed not to offend.
All those years of work undone with the stroke of a pen.
And so I waited and waited for the promise of royalties ordained,
but alas as far as the pennies promised, nothing ever came.

Livid I returned only to see to see another he was stalking,
they were engrossed in conversation; I could see them talking.
so I pricked my ear so as to understand his words,
and after careful deliberation, this is what I heard.

"Jason your unique what a wondrous sound,
what a great and fabulous talent I have found,
there's no one like you, we will make rivers of gold,
promise me your song I promise thousands of copies sold".

Cannon Fodder

Why treasure Napoleon, Hitler, Stalin, and Churchill,
murderers of innocent children.
Why celebrate those who killed thousands,
who murdered brave souls in their millions.

Using proud words, cunning and nationalistic fear,
precious life is transformed into endless graveyards,
so they can test their latest military idea.

While brave grenadiers are needlessly dying,
proudly holding the line,
back in complete safety Churchill smokes his cigar,
Hitler dines, Stalin drinks the finest of wines.

And don't think for a minute they care or can feel your pain.
For these are the true traitors of humanity,
understanding success only by their blood-soaked stains.

Jessica

She said I am the ocean dissolve in me

Who Made the Rain?

Hear the rolling growl of thunder,
did you see the jagged edges of vivid white lightning?
The rain starts to fall.

Tears on my window, fragile silver droplets,
so tiny, so delicate, so small.

Why does it fall, have you asked yourself?
do you ever wonder why?
Is it that God sees the endless needless suffering
and it wounds him so deeply he can't help but cry?

www.ingramcontent.com/pod-product-compliance
Lightning Source LLC
Chambersburg PA
CBHW021140260726
48656CB00023B/1065